Iaroslav Wise

Glimpses of Inspiration

Each person, with God's help, is capable of achieving a lot of positive, useful and important things, be it in science, sports, art, work, studies or other areas. Sometimes, however, we are told "no" too many times or we may be tired of a lot of everyday duties that slow us down instead of helping achieve our objectives. At times, therefore, what may be needed is a little inspiration to proceed and to complete our worthy undertaking. This book does just that – it consists of short poems and picturesque landscapes making us ponder about edifying things and switch to positivity, courage, faith, hope and love to accomplish our kind tasks.

Wise, I. (2022). *Glimpses of inspiration*. Calgary, AB: Edocation Corp.

ISBN 978-1-989531-37-2

Format:	book (paperback)
Language:	English
Written & designed by:	Iaroslav Wise
Published by:	Edocation Corp.
Disclaimer:	this book is published as has been submitted by the author and in the original languages

Acknowledgements

Thank God.

Thank you to my family for their loving support.

Thank you to readers for using and sharing these poems to glorify our Lord and Saviour Jesus Christ and the Holy Trinity.

TABLE OF CONTENTS

THANKSGIVING

Thank You, o God, for all

Thank You, o God, for all,
Thank You for the passing year
Because I had no call;
Thank you for the peace in every sphere.

In order not to drop,
Please, send us wisdom and relief
And also hope in order not to stop;
Please, send us love to get over any reef.

Friday 31.12.2004

I ran a temperature and it is high

I ran a temperature and it is high.
This time, the meaning is direct.
I could've become deaf or even die –
Bad was the illness in fact.

Just as the sea is beneath and the sky is above a region,
Perhaps, my disease was given,
As a message, as a homing pigeon,
To revise my way of life, sometimes so uneven.

I took medicine, I prayed
And I was trying to find the clue.
I saw so many mistakes I had made,
But Jesus Christ saved me and cured, it's true.

So, maybe, the purpose of some maladies is
To give us a chance to realize
That something is wrong, but the hint is like a breeze.
Thank Thee Father, Thou art wise.

Sunday 18.03.2007

Gratitude for all

It is easy to be grateful when all is well,
But to appreciate and thank
When something doesn't "sell"
Is what adds to our "blessing bank".

There are always things to thank for,
And there are also some to pray about to change.
Let sincere, courageous, loving, and hopeful be our core.
A faithful person gets blessings and then again, but more.

Sunday 08.05.2022

He who's never been unthankful

He who's never been unthankful
Will be given his due.
For this, you need so little – true.
Remember this and never be hateful.

Sunday 21.11.2004

Setbacks are not for worrying about

Setbacks are not for worrying about,
But for becoming more stout.

4

Pray and praise the Lord with a heart sincere
And He will make you go far, not near.

Wednesday 23.03.2022

Thank You

I have ears and eyes,
Legs and hands as well.
My dream grows and flies…
Thank You, Father, for each victorious bell!

I have so much, indeed,
And even more,
So that any mortal can only dream of it.
You have so much for us in store!

Thank You for the branch of peace,
For the kind people around,
For the clear air and geese…
You always keep Your servants sound!

Thanks are not enough –
I am to practise good deeds.

Even though waters around are rough,
Your support is all my soul needs!

Friday 17.08.2007

I wish I were sage!

I wish I were sage!
I would know how to deal with rage;
I would avoid all traps;
To benefit I'd turn my mishaps.

I wish I felt sure acting fast
Without crying over the past,
Then I would learn how to mend,
How to improve things on land.

But a wish is not enough to succeed –
I must learn to work hard, indeed.
Thank Thee Father, for giving abilities,
Thank Thee for possibilities!

Sunday – Monday 27–28.07.2008

Oh God, all your creations are good!

Oh God, all your creations are good!
The blue sky, signing birds, fresh air, tasty food…
You support with friendly advice;
From dark earth you bring nutritious rice…

Thank you, Father, for taking care of all:
Us, humans, animals, plants, things big and small.
I know You love everyone.
Thanks to You I accomplished my plans and won!
                    Sunday 25.08.2013

Thank You Father for all the support!

Thank You Father for all the support!
You send me all: life, health, food, creativity!
You navigate me safely to a port.
You show to me the beauty of life in the infinity!
                    Sunday 03.06.2012

LOVE

A moment in a hundred years

I haven't got much money, true,
But a moment in a hundred years
To be with you, to wipe off your tears, –
That's what I've got for you.'

I know that you deserve much more,
Who can tell me why I still hope
And why I keep believing despite the "nope"?
Only God can help me to keep the score.

In spite of all, I can't forget you,
And a moment in a hundred years
To be with you, to forget our fears, –
That's what I've got for you…

Saturday 19.03.2005

8

I need to see you

I really need to see your eyes and face,
But I'm looking for a suitable place.
I want it for my broken heart.
Why is it so? Why do we part?

Friday – Saturday 27–28.02.2004

Feelings are like colours

Feelings are like colours of life,
Like a rainbow with hundreds of shades.

9

They are sharper than a knife
And thinner than blades.

People never know what is behind the hill –
The future is really obscure.
Feelings can hurt or abate will,
But also bring to life or cure.

I don't want to destroy,
So, I must be careful with feelings.
I've realized they are not a toy.
As words in a dictionary, they can have a lot of meanings.

Saturday 04.06.2005

I know that I was wrong

I know that I was wrong,
But is it too late?
The silence is too long.
I have broken my plate,

And you have broken my heart.
I do hope you'll come back

10

And take the leading part
Making whole again our "pack".

My life is like a music show;
You ought to be my DJ:
Your music makes my worry low,
But now I'm just at bay…

Sunday 01.12.2013

Respect yourself!

Respect yourself!
What for to put your talent onto a shelf?
Just find your place,
You are kind that is the fact to face.

You are better than you think!
Your wit is the clue, loving heart is the link.
What are you good at?
Open your mind and develop that!

Tuesday – Saturday 02–06.10.2007

I want to forget all the vanity

I want to forget all the vanity,
And my heart will rejoice for real;
My eyes will clear up seeing sanity.
That's my soul's appeal.

But, oh, how difficult it is –
Let's do it together.
Alone won't do even if we work as hard as bees,
All by myself I am like a torn out feather…

Tuesday 13.02.2007

I know, I have no wings

I know, I have no wings and cannot fly,
But faith, hope and love teach me to,

Even if my hands were full with heavy stuff,
I can, indeed, so high…
Sunday 22.07.2007

One day my parents met each other

One day my parents met each other –
Thank Thee, Gracious Father!

They were young and full of hope,
Their hearts beat like one, as if bound with a rope.

I know, it was love at first sight,
Real love, clear and bright.

Every year succeeded another,
Now my parents have me and my brother.

A lot of things have changed;
Since then much has been rearranged.

Some people say that love is an emotion which perishes –
I don't believe, – real love never vanishes.

Everyone has problems, life is more than a field of rye.
Real love will live, but never die.
Monday 28.11.2005

Stick together

Today the sky is dark,
But everything doesn't depend on weather.
And I enter the empty park.
I wish we were together.

I still remember your last kiss,
If we want, there is nothing that we cannot mend
We will win, we won't miss.
Did we have anything or did we pretend?

Saturday 24.04.2004

Forget about your fears

Forget about your fears,
Please, don't be so sad.

I am with you, I will wipe off your tears.
Cheer up! It drives me mad.

You are my dearest part,
But now your mood is like gloomy weather.
I need a little smile to cure my heart.
Everything will be alright because we are together!

Saturday 28.02.2004

You don't need money to be rich

You don't need money to be rich,
Love and patience are the timely "stitch".
Money may place under the command of gold.
How easily freedom can now be sold.

Is it possible to find a slave who is happy,
Even if s/he seems to be snappy?
The venom of treasure spreads fast
Conquering all: the future, the present, the past.

However, we are free to choose,
And two ways are open: to win or to lose.

Even if you are caught into a silver net,
You can still quit, the things can still be wisely set!

Sunday 09.09.2007

My house is my castle

My house is my castle,
And it's also my fort –
It isn't a place for hustle,
Here you'll find me in thought.

I'm ready to defend my home,
From its foundation to its dome,
Like a soldier and the one who has nowhere to escape.
I love my family and my landscape.

Sunday 17.10.2004

I appreciate you

It's simple and clear, it's true –
There is no one like you.

I appreciate your every idea;
I respect you, don't fear;
Don't worry – the help is not far, but here.

I believe in your "I can, I will",
And if you need anything more, ask God and be still,
You'll be given, believe, you will.
                              Tuesday 17.10.2006

I wish I had a real friend

I wish I had a real friend
So that we could trust each other;

I'm ready to support him till the end,
And if he needed, I'd be able to go farther.

I need a friend to see his eyes,
But if anything happened, I'd wipe off his tears,
And he wouldn't have to tell me lies
Because friends are used to sharing fears.

I'd never get tired of his company,
We wouldn't be bored together;
He'd come to see me a lot of times, but not too many.
And we'd meet just to have a friendly chat in spite of any
weather.

Sunday 01.12.2013

Handsome is as handsome does

Handsome is as handsome does;
Deeds speak more than verbal buzz.
It is good to talk the truthful talk,
But it's also important to walk the faithful walk.
Wednesday 02.03.2022

Why am I so sad?

Why am I so sad?
I cannot understand.
Perhaps, everything is not so bad,
But my troubles are like sand.

How funny it is:
Your one and only phone call
Could cure my "disease" –
You are my cheer and my goal.

Saturday – Sunday 17–18.07.2004

All I really need is your love

All I really need is your love.
I do hope that one day I'll call you my dove.

Your image is deep in my heart,
But you just pass by and it's so hard.

If you could know what I feel,
What an ordeal…

Ain't it stupid to be mad about you?
Today I give up, but tomorrow, I'm going to try anew!

Saturday 10.01.2004

I see "dew" under your eyes

I see "dew" under your eyes,
But why can no one realize?
However you are not alone, be sure.
Look at the sky, its an open door!

The Father is always with you,
He sees and hears, it's true.
Don't be crestfallen, cheer up,
Pray on, He can refill your cup!

Saturday 27.05.2006

20

I'm sitting at the library, here I am

I'm sitting at the library, here I am.
I hear noise of neither a car nor a tram,
Only turning pages and people's rare talks.
Here time doesn't run, but thoughtfully walks.

Here are intelligent women and men,
Professors and students. What then?
Of course, a lot of books
And a young man in glasses counting rooks.

People often call the place "alma mater*" or...
A soft draught and she enters through the open door.
Like a dream, like a white swan.
I stop reading and can't go on.

There is a dozen books in her hands.
I see nothing, but her, no waters, no lands.
I help her with the door and her printed things.
She smiles and thanks, her voice is the music of a bell that rings.

But as dreams usually do, she disappeared.
I didn't even ask her name. What prevented me, what
interfered?

Since then I come here each day...
I can't describe what I feel, simply can't say.

* Latin for "nourishing mother", this phrase is often used to refer to a university or a different educational institution.
Monday 26.09.2005

There is nothing like true love

There is nothing like true love;
It will thrive, it will live, it will fly like a dove.

Some things are no more the same,
How much they've changed: knowledge, style, fame...,

But love stays on.

The grass seems green, the sky seems blue,
But love doesn't seem – it's true.

The shaky world can break,
But love is real, not fake.

A loving heart will overcome!

Love is the light for the eye,
Precious, flying above all the gold, so high!

Love is a shelter for bodies and souls;
Love does flatten hills, love does fill in holes.

Love is Life!

Saturday 14.06.2008

The good spirit of fraternity

The good spirit of fraternity
Will help us reunite.
It'll bring us to eternity,
It will raise our might.

Flowers will grow,
Grass will be green;
The earth will give its fruit for people to mow.
True peace and love will win.

Tuesday 12.05.2009

It's not just you, just me

It's not just you, just me,
We are creating this poem together.
You're not alone, you are just free.
Heart tenderness is lighter than a feather.

What else shall we write?
Perhaps, that we are also not alone?
God is with us, He'll make you sit tight.
Let's believe. Only to believe means to build of stone.

It's so good to have a friend,
To be not separate, but united.
It's a full stop, but not the end,
Because we are together – we aren't short-sighted.

Saturday 08.04.2006

Keep your health from a young age

When you are young, more than in dime,
In your health you should invest your efforts and time.
Then, when you grow, you will say, "I did, I've won".
Share your wisdom with your daughter and son.

Sunday 16.01.2022

To love means to sacrifice

To love means to sacrifice,
But you get your due

As much as a hundred times twice, –
It ain't false – it's true.

If you do not give,
You must not expect to get.
It's up to you to choose how to live:
To hide your inner light or to enjoy each set*.

You can't eat your cake
And have it.
You can't love and only take.
Another fire makes a candle lit.

Sunset.
Sunday 13.08.2006

Is the world turning around?

Is the world turning around?
Well, it's rather rushing.
Listen, you'll hear the sound.

Is there anything to rely upon?
So many things and so little good –

Only love will never be gone.

So, shall I rely on money?
Never, it's only means.
Only pure love can make my days sunny.
Friday 21.07.2006

To my unknown friend

Dear Friend,

We don't know each other yet,
But I believe, we'll meet.
You'll help and I will be in debt,
Thank you for the kind deed.
I'll try to pay you back,
Though you'll never require.
We'll support each other on the track,
Friendship is above personal desire.
In winter, it is a warming fire,
In summer, it is a cool shade.
Our friendship will grow, but never fade.

With deep respect and love,
Your friend.
2007

"What you have, hold"

"What you have, hold",
So many times I've been told,
But what's going on?
I don't appreciate what I have till it's gone.

It's so easy to lose,
Stay awake, don't even snooze.
A single nod is enough
To see how things are rough.

It's impossible to live without a slip,
Watch or miss your tip.
It's okay to get stuck,
But be careful, don't push your luck!

However often you lost
Or whatever you've learnt from your cost,
It isn't yet too late
To put things straight!

Friday 26.08.2005

Do I have love inside?

Do I have love inside?
Anyway, I wish I had.
It brings you up like a high tide.
It is all good and nothing bad.

Love is what I need,
It will bear, it will cure all.
A shield of wisdom will grow from its seed.
It will bring down a wall.

Love unites;
It fills life with sense.
All dark things run away from its lights;
It will climb over misfortune's fence.

Sunday 04.03.2007

To mother

All you had you gave to me,
Your tears and smile…
For my life to be happy and free.
You forgot about yourself as if for a while.

Sleepless nights were yours –
I enjoyed carefree life.
My problems were hers…
I was safe in strife.

Thank you, Mom,
For your heart so kind.
I am sorry for being so blind…
You are still with my problems on your mind.

Friday 10.04.2009

I dreamed I had a friend

I dreamed I had a friend,
His name was Earnest.
Indeed, he was honest.
"What for to pretend?"

He used to say;
He believed and did much pray.
In return, he wanted the same;
Sincere and true was his fame.

I liked him
And tried to be frank.
It was a dream.
Without Earnest life seemed blank.
Let us be earnest.

Tuesday 05.05.2009

Love God with all your heart

Love God with all your heart,
With all your will and mind.
Do things of love which are a good start.
With people, animals, plants, fish and birds be kind.

Do good as much as you can,
Whether at work, at home or at school.
You are a live, wise man.
Love God and love your neighbour; stay cool!
Sunday 27.07.2014

When you want to do a kind thing, do

When you want to do a kind thing, do,
Do not be stopped by what people may think.

You need a kind heart to break through,
This is your saving link!
Sunday 29.09.2013

Not for applause

Love God, He loves us too.
Fulfill His laws.
They give life and health for me and you.
We are striving for salvation, not for applause.
Sunday 10.11.2013

With love

Do all things with love
And God will send you a peace dove.
No use saying kind words
If your heart is empty, – you will receive no real awards.

You want to help your friend,
It is good, but keep in mind the purpose, the end.
Do kind things with a pinch of love:
Help with moving in or out, pick up a glove…

Sunday 14.04.2013

Love is as love does

Love is as love does
One may look nice outside,
But it may be just fuzz,
There may be too much pride.

Love will show itself in deeds,
Not always in a smile that's wide.
Love is what the first Epistle to the Corinthians, chapter 13,
reads
Do you have love inside?

Monday – Wednesday 24–26.10.2011

Whatever happens and when it rains

Whatever happens and when it rains,
I keep relying on God Who saves.
He is my Light,
And His Commandments are my delight!

Whenever He corrects me,
I should accept to blossom like a cherry tree.
He who loves, educates his child
And keeps the youth's heart from being wild!

O Father! Your Law is Life,
Your Love protects from word and strife.
You are my Light!
I keep Your Loving Word in sight!

Saturday 16.10.2011

By wisdom and love

By wisdom and love,
Not by force is God's power:
He sends a peace dove;
In summer, He sends a shower.

Believe, my friend, and boldly act:
He knows His flock.
Be smart to timely react;
Have faith and love in stock.

Thursday 07.04.2011

Kind people around

There are so many kind people around!
Their voice is spreading a lively sound,
Their hearts make the earth rotate.
It feels good with them to associate!

When the world is about to make you cry,
Recall, keep them in mind.
For them, it is worth saving the world, at least to try.
To their neighbour, they are always kind!

Wednesday – Thursday 09–10.02.2011

HAPPINESS

On God my hopes I fix

How far shall I go before a stop?
I am still on my feet, but I am ready to drop;
I am tired, a lot of difficulties surround me,
I hope I'll have rest in the shadow of that tree.

How far shall I go before I am happy?
It is time to get tired, but I am still snappy.
I am ready to snooze, but I cannot allow this.
I am at a loss, I want to cry for peace.

I won't stop in spite of falling bricks,
Because this way's called life,
And on God my hopes I fix.

2004

If everything is wrong

If now everything is wrong,
And the sky above is grey,
Don't be upset – it won't rain long, –
Stay cool and pray.

Saturday 01.12.2013

Do not quench the fire

Do not quench the fire* –
The positivity inside.

Act faster, stronger, higher,
However high is the tide.

* See also 1Th. 5:19
Saturday 21.05.2022

God, have mercy on us

God, have mercy on us
Please, send us wisdom and good will
And my heart will be filled with gladness thus.
I've made some mistake, but my hope is not lost still.

Nothing can be better than Your grace,
Your love will cure and nourish.
We know You see every little tear on every face,
We are sure – Your vineyard will flourish!

Sunday 18.06.2005

I live today

Another day goes by...
What will tomorrow bring?
I don't know, but I must try
To be wise, – that is the thing.

Yesterday is in the past,
Let it be – I live today,
The present is my vast.
The future is far, the past is farther – what else can I say?

Friday 05.08.2005

Worry less

Worry less, buddy,
Unless you are OK giving power over you to your laddie.

41

Have strength and be healthy instead:
Those add up to wealth and a wise head.

Thursday 05.05.2022

Life is good

Life is good
When it's full of hope,
When you don't look at where you stood,
But love and watch peaceful sheep lope.

Life is wonderful treasure
Presented by our Father, Gracious and Kind.
To crown your life with sincere pleasure:
Faith, hope, love… try to find.

Wednesday 19.10.2005

Songs and humour

Songs, so is humour, are crucial
In all circumstances and one –
Do not hide your light under a bushel.
That's how they acted who've won.

Saturday 09.04.2022

Be able to sincerely smile

Be able to sincerely smile,
However hard you labour,

However tough your ride is to cover a mile,
Share a glimpse of hope with your neighbour.

Tuesday 05.04.2022

What is happiness?

What is happiness?
Does it mean being understood?
I don't know… But your silk kiss
Improves the poorest mood.
Saturday 26.02.2005

The truth, wisdom and sincere prayer

Let us choose
Whatsoever things are true.

This is to win and not to lose,
To feel happy, not blue.

Let us sincerely ask
The Lord to make us wise –
He is the One Who makes us accomplish any task.
He wins who prays and tries.

Saturday 26.03.2022

There is measure, even in being sad

The sun above is bright,
It's filling everything with light –
What a wonderful sight!
Birds are singing so well,
But I can't get it right,
I'm sad, yeah, you never can tell.

I guess, it's OK –
There is a reason today,
Though I won't say.
I live with hope

That I'll be shown my way,
And the Father will level the slope.

Sometimes, it's normal to feel sad,
But if there is a reason, something bad –
Otherwise it's like being mad.
You and me, we can cry, but there is measure,
It's true, lad.
Think about it at leisure.

Wednesday 21.12.2005

It isn't worth being sad

It isn't worth being sad
Because you can be taken bad.
Your smile is your cure.
Look, the sky isn't so obscure!

Come on, be quick!
It's time to click;
Stand up and dance –
Otherwise you risk to miss your chance.

Sunday 02.01.2005

What a wonderful world

I hear birds singing
Their morning wake-up song;
I wake up to see what the day is bringing –
Will it be short or will it be long.

I feel calm and easy,
But have no idea why.
The air is fresh and breezy.
What for to sigh?

I also see a little baby
Comfortably curled.
What for to doubt and to say "maybe" –
It's a wonderful world!

Sunday 19.11.2006

Enjoy life whatsoever

Enjoy life whatsoever.
While you can do good, do it ever.
Let faith, hope, love dispel the word "never".
In studies and work be kindly clever.

Sunday 20.02.2022

On the next day after Pascha

Everything will be all right!
God loves us so much!

48

We sleep, but the Father takes care of us, even at night.
Pray, believe, smile, hold tight!

Monday 09.04.2007

Pascha – what a Day!

Pascha* – what a Day!
Today we rejoice and pray!
Today nature rejoices too!
Today we eat and break through!

* Also known as "Easter".
Saturday (before Pascha) 23.04.2022

You are always asking

You are always asking,
"What am I supposed to do?",
But the answer is inside of you.
Open your eyes, stop masking.

Just kindly do what is in your power
And never stand back
Because that's the right track.
Believe. you can reach the top of the tower!
Saturday 10.07.2004

What are you looking for

What are you looking for,
Money, power and fame?

Hurry up, be sure,
Flowing water is never the same.

Faith, hope and love?
Choose, it's up to you,
Either a white dove
Or worry and the mood that's blue.
Monday – Tuesday 04–05.06.2007

Every moment

He should savour every minute of life,
But rudeness in his manners is growing rife.

He has feet, ears, eyes and hands,
But can't understand where he stands.

This man has so much,
But doesn't want to see and it's his personal touch.

He has never seen a rifle,
But worries about every trifle.

Peace is better than strife.
He should savour every moment of life.
Saturday – Saturday 12.02–05.03.2005

I am so happy to live

I am so happy to live.
Though this life is transient like a sun ray,
And I will have to take leave,
I am so happy today!

I am happy!
How many kind things I can do!
I am young and snappy,
And I will break through!

Thank You, Father, for life,
Both for the present and for that.
Green grass, freedom and love… LIFE!
I bow and take off my hat.

Saturday 27.09.2008

Life is good (2)

Life is good.
Be strong to face it.
He'll see who can change his mood.
Life is a miracle, wherever you place it.

Life is the most generous gift –
Can't you still realize?
Till it's not too late again, be swift.
Soften your heart, you will see rise.
Sunday 01.12.2013

Less time on the phone

Wise people spend less time on the phone
And more on the world that's real,

More on relationships and quality communication,
Less on news and social media frustration.

Monday 24.01.2022

Circumstances to blame? A sparkle inside

Are circumstances to blame?
People suffer feeling pain.
Where is the inner flame?
A silenced song under the rain…

But water from above is okay
When the soul is alive,
When the strings of you play.
Your business is going to thrive

Because you have nothing to blame
Simply and wisely walking your way.
Perhaps <u>here</u> is hidden people's fame,
'A sparkle inside', you might say.
                    Wednesday 18.03.2009

Worry not – God is with you

Never worry – God is above all.
When you pray, He hears your call.
Your task is small: to keep wisely rolling your ball,
To spread your shoulders and to stand tall.

Sunday 16.01.2022

To worry or not to worry, that is the question

There are only 365 days or so in a year,
And there are limited years in this life.

What is the number that's fair
To sacrifice to worry, to cut those days out as if with a knife?

Maybe, three or four…? How about none?
How about spending those to God's glory
To build, to fly, to support, to swim, to read, to run…
And to make complete and meaningful your story?

Sunday 16.01.2022

How much money do I need?

How much money do I need?
I just want to be happy indeed.
Perhaps, a million will do?
Though, it'll be better to have two.

But I say no, money is never enough,
It cannot make happy, but rough.
The more I'll have, the more I'll need.
It's like a very bad seed.

So, I conclude that love and help to the neighbour
Can bring peace and make flourish my labour.

It is up to me to choose.
I know what to do in order not to lose!

Sunday 21.10.2007

Give up your fear

Give up your fear.
Let your kindness shine.
Help people to be sincere.
This is our call divine.

Let you light reveal to others
That we are all brothers,
That real life is in doing good;
Goodness is not far, it is around, it is in the neighbourhood.

Saturday 29.01.2011

Easy way

You live in fear
Because you have chosen an easy way;
You may not want to hear,
But listen what from my heart I am trying to say…

You risk nothing on this earth:
You will take as much as you have brought.
Look wider at the Universe!
There is much more after this life than you have thought.

Prepare for yourself a better spot.
So many possibilities exist!
Your chances to help people are a lot.
So, choose: to perish on an easy way or to try at least.

Saturday 29.01.2011

Pay it forward

Pay it forward and it will pay back:
You will have enough and will not lack;
You will change the world around;
You will make your business safe and sound.

Friday 07.01.2022

Because you have life

Smile, all is gonna be okay,
It is a wonderful day!

Today is time to win,
Put all your misfortunes into the bin.

Smile, I admire your strength,
Your success is longer than length.
You can win in the strife.
Smile because you have life!

Monday 19.04.2010

STUDIES & WORK

Not all dreams

Not all dreams are to be chased by thee,
But there are those that should be.
Be wise and discern;
Be faithful and learn.

Tuesday 05.07.2022

Do not open up at work

Do not open up at work,
At desk or at cork.

Also keep it professional and simple;
To cope with tasks and succeed, use your dimple.
Friday 01.07.2022

People differ

There is a temptation
To think about one as all,
But people differ in every team and nation.
So, be wise, attentive to enter the communication fame hall.
Saturday 18.06.2022

The stuff we do matters

The stuff we do matters,
Presidents, housewives, hatters…

Therefore, do good and be wise
When it comes to important stuff – do not compromise.
Saturday 11.06.2022

It is possible to be with money, but poor

It is possible to be with money, but poor.
Not sure? Travel, take a tour.
What makes us rich is what's in our heart.
Make kind deeds your every day's part.
Sunday 29.05.2022

Focus

It may be difficult to concentrate
When there is so much going on around,

But try to focus on one thing at a time.
Let it be slow, but do not procrastinate.
The ones who sought are the ones who found.
The morning is the period of day that's prime.
Work on, prioritize, climb.

Sunday 15.05.2022

How easy it is to sink in a marsh

How easy it is to sink in a marsh,
I mean in everyday vanity:
Just a step from a crush
Of good sense, of sanity.
Fuss is like the vacuum of space,
Like emptiness which swallows up mass,
All things at a steady pace,
It's like ruin spreading out as if it were gas.
That's the way it often is,
But what shall I do?
God, help me, please.
I don't want to vanish in nothing, in ado
Saying, "What shall we eat?"*

"What shall we drink?" or what to put on our feet?
Our heavenly Father knows that we need all these things and what's meet.
So, let's seek first the kingdom of God and His righteousness truly
And all these things shall be added to us timely and fully.
Thank You, Father!

See Mt. 6:31-33.
Sunday 09.07.2006

Guard your mouth

Guard your mouth at all times.
That will save you nerves and limes.
When you speak,
Take time, make wisdom and simplicity the stuff you seek.

Tuesday 03.05.2022

You are tired of their envy

You are tired of their envy.
You worked a lot and won,
But they consider you an enemy.
Don't worry, they can do nothing. No one!

Relax, keep your chin up,
Show them your winning smile.
They are already wound up,
So, they are weak, take your chance, cover your mile.

Saturday 26.06.2004

I am tired, I work a lot

I am tired, I work a lot;
I've done so much,

Though much more is left to touch –
It is like someone's plot.

Something is wrong,
It's like an unfinished song.
I have to change in a sort –
Life is too short.

Saturday 23.10.2004

What is essential in life

What is essential in life,
Money or friendship,
Aloofness or strife?

The answer seems to be clear,
But do my actions support
What my mind declares now and here?

I want to find the true way,
It's covered with thorns, not flowers, I know,
While the sun shines I should make hay.

Friday 01.12.2006

Be wise – there is no time to yawn

You've lost a round,
So what? The game is going on.
Think about what you've found;
Now you are stronger, be wise – there is no time to yawn.

Of course, you can stall and not be sure,
And also give in and not fight,
But look, how many goals are left for you to score!
Isn't it better to keep your chin up? Aren't you young and
bright?

Saturday 12.03.2005

Nights are getting colder

Nights are getting colder;
Time is slipping away;

Your young heart has become older,
And it has nowhere to stay.

You've made a big career
From a boy to a well-known banker;
But life is not all work, oh hear:
It's not enough to be a ranker.

Your money is naught
When your heart is lone.
Remember this thought,
Perhaps, it's not too late to change the tone.

Sunday 14.11.2004

Your life is perfectly set up

Your life is perfectly set up…
A sheet of paper is thin, so is our chance when we stall.
It's so difficult to climb up,
But it's so easy to fall!
Thursday 30.03.2006

Sometimes we all need a good rest

Sometimes we all need a good rest
To be able to go on with zest,
That is, we shouldn't work too much.
I hope someone will understand because it isn't Dutch.

It does not mean that we should never labour –
Sometimes we just need a good rest:
Rest from the boss and the worker, an exam and a test…
It's written for you and your neighbour.
Saturday 28.05.2005

Instead of a conclusion

Riches and fame are nought.
They can neither make happy

Nor cure, not really support.
They will make no person snappy.

But true love makes whole your soul.
Love gives power in strife
And you score your goal.
Let's choose what leads to life.

Friday 31.03.2006

Work without overworking

It is good to work hard,
But to overwork is not –
On this one, you can trust the bard.
For health, faith, hope and love, stay on guard.

Saturday 12.02.2022

You are free at last

You are free at last,
This is another weekend;
Your prime isn't past;
Optimism and lightness always trend.

So, spread your shoulders and smile.
You will stand and all issues will scatter.
Let wise, loving, courageous, hopeful and faithful be your style.
Relax and you'll feel better.

Saturday 15.11.2003

Be patient

Be patient when you write an email – reread;
Be patient with your colleagues and clients if you want to succeed;

Be patient with your family, friends, pet if you would like to lead.
If you lack it – ask the Lord to give to safely proceed.
Friday 04.02.2022

They want you to do all

They want you to do all,
So much load to carry, indeed.
"Keep on!", they say when you fall.
Though silent, your ever-young heart does bleed.

Calm down, I beg you,
No load is worth you.
They may be blind, but you see;
You can choose the way to be free.

He who refuses to see,
Risks health in the world of the blind,
Hurts himself and may be condemned to flee.
Being with them is to lose,
Being wise is to find.
Thursday 16.10.2008

73

Boss vs leader

It is bad to be a boss,
But it's good to lead:
The former means health and relationship loss,
The latter plants a good seed.

Friday 21.01.2022

Keep your health

A house is built from its base.
To achieve good stuff, start work without laze,

But it is your health that is the core –
Keep it if you want to achieve more.
Sunday 16.01.2022

Too much of one thing is good for nothing

Too much of work sometimes result in fruits that are few.
As soon as that is done, there is more work anew.
Working too little is also undue.
Balance, therefore, is the way to go, in my view.
Sunday 16.01.2022

When the small things of everyday pass

When the small things of everyday pass,
What will remain?

What makes out of nothing a mess?
What is main?

Our worries (job, studies) and fears change in a wink.
God is Eternal.
It's never too late to think
And align your life with things supernal.
Monday – Thursday 15–18.05.2011

If you are lazy, pray

If you are lazy, pray,
Because a lazy soul will suffer hunger and thirst.
There is time to work and time to play,
But let our duty go first.

Christian people are meek and hard-working,
By their work they build themselves a house;
Their men are surrounded by their family and have the best wine
to uncork;
Their women wear the best silk blouse.

Let us pray and work with zest
For we work for our own reward,
At least, let us try to do our best.
Sunday 22.09.2013

COURAGE

With courage, faith and hope

When you fail,
There'll be those who support
And those who top it up with hail,
But you, of courage, faith and hope never fall short.

Monday 27.06.2022

You have to believe

You have to believe,
Not only when all looks good,

But even when you scramble to earn food.
God is with you and will never leave.
Monday 27.06.2022

Always keep faith and hope

Always keep faith and hope –
No matter what, with God's help you can cope.
Let your love be true and sincere,
Let your speech and writing be clear.
Saturday 11.06.2022

Be clever

Whatever happens, life goes on,
The things will improve before long.

78

No misfortune can last forever,
But this life is for once, so why not to be clever?

I already see winning lights,
They are shining in your street scattering nights.
The past is to learn from, the future is obscure,
But the present requires of us to be wise and to endure.

The support is not far,
It will come like a glowing star.
Then be ready to accept it at once,
Be ready in order not to miss your chance!

Wednesday 29.08.2007

Flowers are growing

Flowers are growing;
The Earth is going around;
Wind is blowing;
Movement... Even silence seems to have some sound.

Like the running water of a stream,
Life is likely to change;

It always looks for a beam.
Who can never stumble in the long eventful range?

There is one thing to remember:
It is never too late to improve;
It often rains in September;
To succeed we need to be wise and to move.

Sunday 03.12.2006

Proceed with caution, courage and wisdom

Proceed with caution, courage and wisdom, indeed.
Be faithful, loving and gentle in every word and deed.
Stay your true Christian self,
Whether you are a soldier, a teacher, a priest or fill a store shelf.

Saturday 09.04.2022

It's not easy, but go on

It's not easy, but go on:
It's easy to give up, but it's difficult to fight.
Misfortunes cannot last long,
Be ready for light.

You try to do good,
But they have no clue…
I know, it's ungrateful, it's rude.
Be sure, you'll be given your due.
Sunday 02.07.2006

Never give up the fight

It is easy to be deceived
And to miss what you might have received –

A faithful victory, man.
Therefore, be wise and have a plan.

Tuesday 05.04.2022

We ought to believe

We ought to believe
Not only when all is well, but alway.
Those who seek, receive.
God will make a way!

Saturday 12.03.2022

About God's grace never doubt

About God's grace never doubt.
Light is the thing to focus on – sit tight.

82

All that you can do, do; do not give up the ball.
Be smart and humble and from there depart.

Sunday 06.03.2022

Nothing is impossible when you believe

Nothing is impossible when you believe
Because you will not hesitate, you will never grieve.

But to believe does not mean just to wait –
It means to study, to work and only then to anticipate.

"Faith without works is dead".*
It's true, what else can be said?

So, pray for success and keep on rowing;
Your business will flourish and will be happily flowing.

Hesitation is not for you,
You will overcome, you will break through.

* See Jm.2:20; Mk. 9:23.
Sunday 08.07.2007

Whatever happens, believe

Whatever happens, believe,
However high the waves are:
Remember, you will retrieve,
Just keep on going so far.

It's easy to lose hope,
To say, "I will never be forgiven".
It's not true, it's a slippery slope.
Lazy is he who has never striven.

Believe if you don't want to fall.
Believe if you want to win.
Despair is not good at all,
It rather looks like a sin.

Faith will improve the things,
Be brave enough to act.
Spread your little wings,
You are strong, in fact.

Sunday 21.01.2007

In dreams I can see a green lawn

In dreams I can see a green lawn,
A calm, not very deep river, so clear,
As if peace and quiet here were born,
And the blue sky is so near...

However, it is time to wake up,
Dreams can't last too long.
But who said I cannot make up?
Who said I cannot be strong?

Life has only just begun.
All I need is to try to be clever
To see God's sun
And a horizon that goes on forever...

Friday – Saturday 06–07.10.2006

A truthful man will stand

A truthful man will stand,
Unlike the one who stumbles, because he is unsure,
In air, at sea, on land,
A kind man will stand.

But he, who has no kind deed to declare
Risks to fall from a blow,
He who lives on hesitation that is unclear
Should understand that his plans won't go far, but near.

Oh, how time is flying!
And yet, there is time to renew,
To open your heart to love, to morning dew,
And you will find that it's true!

Saturday 04.10.2008

Life is too short for saying "too late"

He had friends, money and fame.
Bad luck changed it to nothing, but shame.
At magnificent parties he ate his bread,
But now he went hungry to bed.

He tasted much of meekness;
However tired or thirsty, he never settled for weakness.
He began from the start,
"The life is long, and small is my part".

He stood the blow and did not cry,
The guy had the courage to say "I'll try".
The wisdom regained him all and even more!
"Be honest, do good and you'll win, for sure…"

Saturday 30.08.2008

When I sincerely ask

When I sincerely ask,
Our Father graciously gives,
For little me He solves any task,
And so my soul lives.

When I am in trouble,
Our Father sends me support.
My problems crack like a bubble,
And I win a medal, just like in sport.

Thursday 26.11.2009

I expect one thing

I expect one thing,
But other things arrive.

What the next minute will bring?
How strange it is, what a rapid drive!

I was ready for a delay,
But the bus didn't come at all.
I was going to play,
But had to work because of a call.

"Do not worry about tomorrow
For tomorrow will worry about its own things"*.
Cares produce only sorrow,
Why to clip our heart's wings?

I hope I shall look firmly ahead
And shall not be unwise,
But confident instead.
It's not for me: cares and plans of enormous size.

See also Mt. 6:34.
Saturday 15.04.2006

Come on, "victory" say!

Come on, "victory" say!
"We'll win" cry out!

Keep your chin up, hey!
You will have much good today!

This is your morning, your time.
You need no hesitation.
So, enjoy today's prime.
Smile to avoid a lime.

Be active now
Because this leads to success.
Let puppies say "bow-wow" –
You should walk your way, you know how!

Saturday 10.05.2008

Hey, what a sad face!

Hey, what a sad face!
Don't worry, everything's gonna be all right;
Take it easy and you'll win the race;
The rainy day will go away and you will see the light!

Smile and the world will smile with you.
If you want to feel better, try to move or dance,

It really helps, it's true.
The life is going on, don't miss your chance.

There is no doubt,
Your problems will blow like a chewing gum bubble,
Just believe and be stout.
A kind heart will never be left in trouble.

Wednesday 03.08.2005

When speeches are truthless

When speeches are truthless,
When the spirits are low,
Do not be afraid of your foe.
Cowing of the weak is all they are able to show.

Every word intending to bite…
Keep your chin up – you are right.
You were born not for a crawl, but for a flight.
You have chosen the way of love and light.

Whatever they do, be wise, be yourself.
Cruel arrows will break;

Far and deep will stretch your lake.
So, remain brave, be awake.
Sunday 07.09.2008

Do not fear, little flock

Do not fear, little flock:
Your Lord is with you.
You are better than an ant although it works around the clock,
But even it is not forgotten by your Father.
Be brave, pursue your goal anew, have faith in stock.
Sunday 27.04.2014

Believe in God, trust in Him and go!

Believe in God, trust in Him and go!
Let your spirits be high, not low.

Believe in God and act;
May He give you wisdom to react!

Sunday 24.11.2013

Rely on God, be brave!

Rely on God, be brave!
You will achieve your goal.
You won't be a slave;
You will eat the food which is whole.

Let's thank God for what we have and let's work for more;
Let us use our brain and skills
To receive a better score,
To pay our daily bills.

When hardships arrive,
Let us pray to God to work them out
By wisdom, love and deeds which are live.
Let us rely on God to be happy and stout!

Sunday 14.07.2013

Rely on God, don't worry

Rely on God, don't worry.
In life, you may have some struggle –
No need to hurry –
Otherwise, it will grow like a bubble.

Rely on God, don't worry.
Just do what you can do;
Do not be sorry.
No doubt, you will break through!

Rely on God, don't worry.
However serious the situation is,
Even if it's health or money…
Do not give up and smile, please! :)

Sunday 02.10.2011

Have faith in a storm to stand

Have faith in a storm to stand,
You will overcome.
However hard to understand…
Your Protector is High; you are strong without rum.

You know it all.
Look deeper in your heart.
You will feel a kindness call;
Of the best in the world you are a part.

Sunday 16.01.2011

As we grow up

Today you are fourteen,
Rejoice, my friend:

Your way is wide, your soul is keen!
But what does it mean to win in the end?

Choose your aim,
You may have several of them...
So that your heart does not blame;
Be captain of your helm.

You can win;
Be brave, my friend.
Although some will greet it with a grin,
Keep in mind the end.

Tuesday 28.12.2010

Your heart is brave

Your heart is brave,
Your brain is smart.
To live, to help, to save
Is your part.

Your smile can cure;
Your hug is warm.
Though you have to endure,
Your patience, love and work will calm down the storm.

Tuesday 08.06.2010

MISCELLANEOUS

Follow the Light

Follow the Light;
Jesus Christ is the Way, the Truth, the Life*.
Keep you mind bright.
Keep kind deeds and wisdom in sight.
Jn. 14:6.
Tuesday 05.07.2022

Be faithful in any situation

Be faithful in any situation,
In your own and any other nation,
In abundance and deprivation,
Through easy times and at time of temptation.
Monday 27.06.2022

Be patient, be nice and sincere

Be patient, be nice and sincere.
Seek wisdom and you will find.
Make your communication gentle and clear.
Keep bright your heart and your mind.

Thursday 02.06.2022

A tradition

He's got a tradition
Of doing something good at least once a week.

I think, it doesn't need a permission.
Isn't it good to help those who are weak?

I don't know why,
But one day he lost all he had.
It just happened, but he didn't cry.
He lost his house, but said that it wasn't still so bad.

Guess what happened then.
He'd been giving, but they turned back upon him,
They refused. They! Not one, but ten.
He still believed in God, his faith didn't dim.

"It might still have been worse",
He used to say.
"Not all minds are coarse…"
The man could hardly find a place where to stay.

"Don't you remember?"
A young man addressed him.
And he recognised his timbre.
The old man didn't show that he was crying, he only touched his
rim.

"I remember your tradition.
Thank God, we've met; I hope I can help you."
"You don't have to, I am in a fair condition…"
Oh, how important the deeds that are true!

Saturday 15.10.2022

I didn't think when I had to

I didn't think when I had to.
I acted quickly, it's true,
But now I realize
The weight of the issue, its size.

Look with your heart and your eyes.
The sun will soon rise.
Look before you leap
If you don't want to regret,
If you don't want to sink deep.
Saturday 18.03.2006

Salt and light

You are the salt,
You are the light*.

In good deeds, don't halt.
Keep all God's Commandments always in sight.

See Mt. 5:13-14
Saturday 23.04.2022

He spends all the time with his back to the wall

He spends all the time with his back to the wall;
His guitar touches the strings of hearts.
He is young and he is on the ball.
His music helps those who are in the cart.

Each sound is a feeling;
Each note is a sincere word.
For those who are suffering, this music is healing,
It's telling of something they've never yet heard.

Saturday 05.03.2005

What is life?

What is life?
Who can tell?
Is it all peace and quiet or strife?
Anyway, there is no time for us to sell.

One must be swift to realize
That time is quick.
That's where another open secret lies
And it's better to be smart and sane, not sick.

Life is an incredible wonder.
It's up to each person to choose,
But there is little time to ponder.
You <u>can</u> be careful and wise if you don't want to lose.

Saturday – Sunday 25–26.11.2006

The thoughts on a rainy day

What a rainy day;
You hear light snaps outside.
How much you could say,
But the thoughts are muffling the words like a tide.

The present, the future and the past,
They walk hand in hand at once.
The first one is alive. Gone is the one that's last.
The future is only a possible chance.
Sunday 15.10.2006

Just a poem

You often go past a young man
Whose guitar tells you more than songs can.

103

Do you think that he is a poor guy?
No, he is much richer than you.
He isn't a TV star, but it doesn't make him cry.
You say that his possessions are few,

Perhaps… Yes, he lives on his dreams,
But no one can take them away
Because they are just like gleams,
Gleams of hope and God is his only stay.

So, never say that he is weak, –
He is getting stronger week after week.
Saturday 08.01.2005

Let us do what we can, each one in our own place

We may be unable to change it all,
But if we respond to the call
To do what is in our power,
One day we may wake to a successfully built tower.
Wednesday 23.03.2022

Here is the author's feather

Here is the author's feather.
What will it write about, nasty or good weather?
Will it praise or will it not?
Where will it draw a full stop?

Wednesday 15.12.2005

Grown-ups are oftener right than I thought

Grown-ups are oftener right than I thought,
By own mistakes I was taught.

105

Why does it take so much time:
Stubbornness only takes away dime.

Now I see it in the mirror of the past,
But I don't cry, I say "at last"!

And do you know why?
Listen, here is some wisdom – not far, but nigh:

If you adopt good,
You will succeed, what for to be in a bad mood?

You'd better be sage:
Be patient and respect any age.
Sunday 17.06.2007

How to win and crystalize your victories

Steady wins the race;
Patient wins the prize;
Tidy makes healthy the place;
Loving and faithful makes victories crystalize.
Saturday 29.01.2022

The nights are getting colder…

The nights are getting colder…
A lot of efforts seem to be in vain,
But he is becoming bolder
And sage under the rain.

Having nowhere to go
And no one to pity,
Though sometimes a bit low,
He is always courageous and witty.

Brain and muscles to earn bread…
"It's not for life", he says.
Never has he fled.
"I'll try and they will come, sunny days".

No one seems to hear,
So, he closes his eyes.
His better future is near, –
Hope and good will never lie.

Saturday 05.07.2008

He who wants to gain by lies

He who wants to gain by lies
Is cheating himself,
He has tiny luck, however much he tries
And no jam on the shelf.

It is simple and true,
Though tough to understand.
Everyone is getting his due,
His prize in his hand.

Look around to see.
God will give you to drink.
Wisdom and love abide to make you free.
Before stepping, just think.

Tuesday – Tuesday 26.05–02.06.2009

Freedom is given

Freedom is given;
You are free to choose.
Who seeks will be forgiven.
He was free, but didn't lose.

Sunday 04.10.2009

One thing to remember

One thing to remember:
You are beautiful and strong,

December through November.
Listen to the Church bell song.

Be sure, just wisely go,
You'll see the sunrise.
Let your faith grow
Striving for the eternal prize.

October 2009

Look before you leap

Look before you leap,
Try to analyze.
Wisdom is deep,
Early is a magnificent sunrise!

You can plan in advance.
Believe in God and take your chance.
Do it to be firm on your way,
You will walk on a bright day.

Sunday 05.07.2009

Time as finances

If you think about your days as a precious dime,
How would you like to invest your time?
Worry, by the way, is like a "stealing crime";
Doing nothing is asking to increase your "mortgage prime".

How about education –
The "metal" that always grows in evaluation,
Or family hours – the "real estate" bringing a dividend despite inflation?
For savings and tax deductions, consider prayer, love, donation.

Sunday 16.01.2022

The world is like a maze

The world is like a maze:
So easy to get lost

Trying to find the base!
Be ready to pay a wise cost.

We run risks and win,
We invest and harvest,
But they who do nothing, but grin
Are going to lose all without the rest.

I have the brain to think,
I have the heart to love and to like.
These are a real link
To well-being in this life hike!

Saturday 17.05.2008

Freedom of speech

If you live in a place
Where all sorts of sinful stuff are "okey",
But healthy, peaceful Christian practices are off lips, off face –
This is not freedom of speech – keep believing and pray.

Friday 18.09.2020

Communication

It is important for every nation
To live in peace and quiet:
Plain heart communication
Is like other things that are right:

Clear air to breathe;
Fresh food to eat…
Honest words are like honey of bees –
Use only them whenever you meet.

Tuesday 14.07.2009

Be frank wherever you are

Be frank wherever you are;
Positive confidence will take you so far;

A pure heart can open doors;
You will run up many floors.

Be yourself, try,
Look up in the sky so high.
Do good, let people admire.
Youth is as warm as fire.

Sunday – Monday 28–29.06.2009

Her enemy is sometimes her tongue

Her enemy is sometimes her tongue.
Wordiness and lies may seem sweet –
About it a lot of trumpets sung,
On both, posh carpet and deserted street.

The truth may seem bitter or salty,
But the Earth is round,
And some things under the moon are faulty.
We know only one Place where no mistakes are found.

But the thing is,
It's not worth while speaking much.

114

A word can sting worse than bees.
Let each sound be with wisdom's touch.
Tuesday 20.09.2005

When something is wrong, speak up

When something is wrong, speak up.
If you are doing something good, do not give up!
Let your kind deeds to others shine.
I believe in you, you can achieve it all without wine!
Saturday – Monday 14–16.06.2014

When I go to Church

When I go to Church,
Something strange arrives:

My studies green like a young birch,
And my creativity thrives…

September 2011

When something is not the way you'd like

When something is not the way you'd like,
It's time to think:
Let rest the mike,
Take time, postpone the rink.

Rely on God and you will see,
The things will change:
Win-win for thee;
For others – simply strange.

Saturday 07.05.2011

Practise what you preach

Practise what you preach
And you will feel so light;
You will increase your reach;
People will find you fair and bright!
Saturday 16.04.2011

It's just the beginning

It's just the beginning,
It's not the end:
Birds will be signing,
You will find a friend,

You will live together
And will support each other,
No matter what's the weather,
Your life will be winning!

Monday 19.07.2010

Index (tags)

Reader's notes